Kid's Box

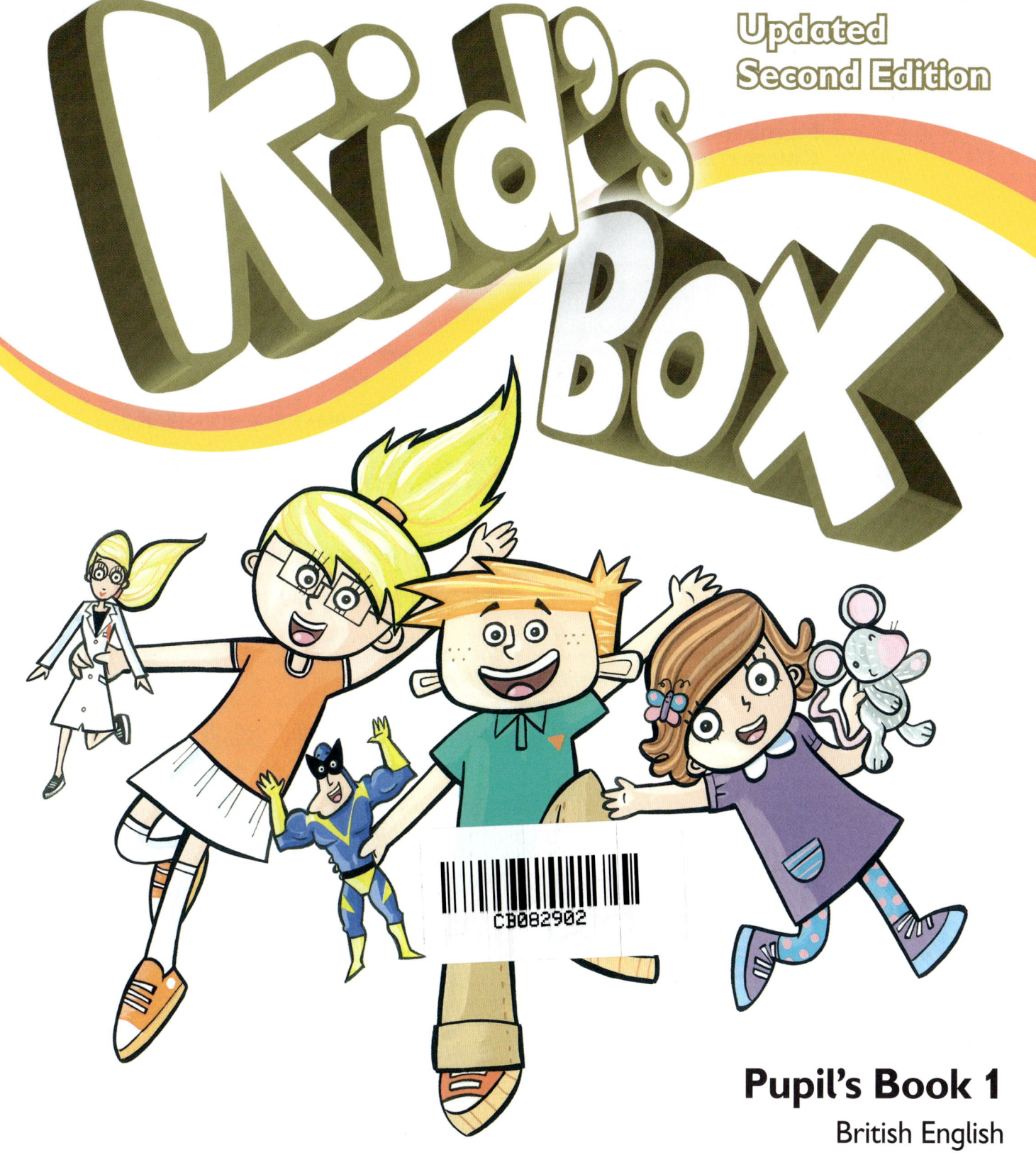

Updated Second Edition

Pupil's Book 1

British English

Caroline Nixon & Michael Tomlinson

Language summary

		Key vocabulary	Key grammar and functions	Phonics
1	**Hello!** page 4	**Character names:** Mr Star, Mrs Star, Stella, Simon, Suzy, Marie, Maskman, Monty, Meera **Numbers:** 1–10 **Colours:** blue, green, pink, purple, red, orange, yellow, rainbow	**Greetings:** Hello, I'm (Stella), Goodbye. What's your name? How old are you? I'm (seven). What colour's (the pencil)? It's (red).	Initial letter sound: 's' (six)
2	**My school** page 10	**School objects:** book, chair, eraser, pen, pencil, table **Character names:** Alex, Lenny	Who's that? He's (Alex). She's (Meera). Who's he/she? How old is he/she? He/She is (six). How are you? I'm fine, thank you.	Initial letter sounds: 'p' and 'b' (pink, blue)

Marie's maths **Adding** page 16   **Trevor's values** **Make friends** page 17

3	**Favourite toys** page 18	**Toys:** ball, bike, car, computer, doll, train **Colours:** black, brown, grey, white	What's your favourite toy? My favourite toy is (a train). Where's (your bag)? Is (your bag) under (your chair)? **Prepositions:** in, next to, on, under	Initial letter sounds: 't' and 'd' (ten, dolls)
4	**My family** page 24	**Family:** brother, sister, father, mother, grandfather, grandmother	We're (young). Who's that? **Adjectives:** beautiful, ugly, happy, sad, old, young	Short vowel sound: 'a' (sad)

Marie's art **Mixing colours** page 30   **Trevor's values** **Be kind** page 31

Review 1 2 3 4 page 32

5	**Our pets** page 34	**Pets:** bird, cat, dog, fish, horse, mouse	They're (small), plurals **Adjectives:** big, small, clean, dirty, long, short	Short vowel sound: 'e' (ten)
6	**My face** page 40	**The face:** ears, eyes, face, hair, mouth, nose, tooth/teeth **Body parts:** head, knees, shoulders, toes	Have you got (a small mouth)? Yes, I have. No, I haven't. I've got (purple hair). We've got (six dirty ears).	Initial consonant blends: 'gr,' 'br' and 'fr' (green, brown, frog)

Marie's science **The senses** page 46   **Trevor's values** **Look after pets** page 47

		Key vocabulary	Key grammar and functions	Phonics
7	**Wild animals** page 48	**Animals:** crocodile, elephant, giraffe, hippo, monkey, snake, tiger **Body parts:** arm, foot/feet, hand, leg, tail	They've got (big mouths). They haven't got (tails). Have they got (long legs)? How many (teeth) have they got?	Short vowel sound: 'i' (s<u>i</u>x)
8	**My clothes** page 54	**Clothes:** jacket, shoes, skirt, socks, (pair of) trousers, T-shirt	He's/She's got (red trousers). He/She hasn't got (a jacket).	Short vowel sound: 'o' (d<u>o</u>g)

Marie's geography | Habitats — page 60   Trevor's values | Love nature — page 61

Review 5 6 7 8 — page 62

		Key vocabulary	Key grammar and functions	Phonics
9	**Fun time!** page 64	**Activities:** play football / basketball / tennis, play the guitar / piano, swim, ride a bike, sing, fish	I/You/She/He can (sing). I/You/She/He can't (drive a car). What can you do? Can you (fish)?	Consonant sound: 'l' (<u>L</u>ily, b<u>l</u>ue)
10	**At the funfair** page 70	**Vehicles:** boat, bus, helicopter, lorry, motorbike, plane, ship	What are you doing? I'm (flying).	Short vowel sound: 'u' (d<u>u</u>ck)

Marie's sports | Things for sports — page 76   Trevor's values | Work in teams — page 77

		Key vocabulary	Key grammar and functions	Phonics
11	**Our house** page 78	**Rooms:** bathroom, bedroom, dining room, hall, kitchen, living room **Activities:** eat fish, watch TV, have a bath	What's he/she doing? He's/She's (listening to music). What are they doing? They're (sitting on the sofa). Is he/she (reading)? Yes, he/she is. No, he/she isn't. **Verb + -ing spellings:** colouring, playing	Initial consonant sound: 'h' (<u>h</u>orse)
12	**Party time!** page 84	**Food:** apple, banana, burger, cake, chocolate, ice cream, kiwi **Activities:** make a cake	I like (cake). I don't like (chocolate). Do you like (snakes)? Yes, I do. No, I don't.	Long vowel sound: 'i_e'/'y' (b<u>i</u>k<u>e</u>, fl<u>y</u>)

Marie's art | Fruit in paintings — page 90   Trevor's values | Keep clean — page 91

Review 9 10 11 12 — page 92   Grammar reference — page 94

1 Hello!

1 🔊 Listen and point.

Stella
Mr Star
Simon
Suzy
Mrs Star

2 🔊 Listen and repeat.

3 Listen and do the actions.

Maskman   Marie   Monty

4 Say the chant.

1 2 3 4 5 6 7 8 9 10

Functions	Vocabulary
Hello, I'm ... What's your name? Goodbye.	1–10

5 🎧 Listen and point.

How old are you?

I'm three.

Meera

6 🎧 Listen and repeat.

Simon 6

Meera 8

Suzy 3

Stella 7

Functions
How old are you? I'm …

7 🔊 🎵 Sing the song.

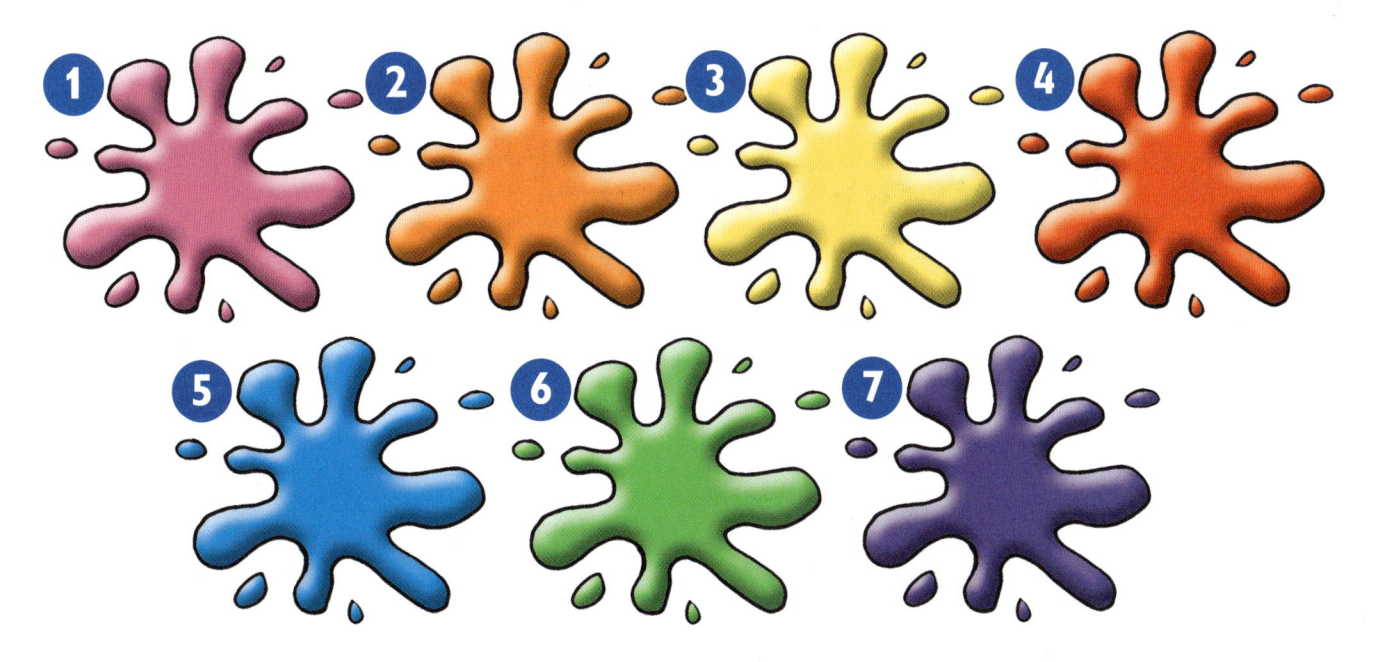

8 🔊 💬 Listen and say the colour.

1 2 3 4

5 6 7

Vocabulary

blue   green   orange   pink   purple   red   yellow

9 **Monty's phonics**

six

star

Six stars.

10 Ask the questions.

What's your name?

How old are you?

Stella 7

Simon 6

Suzy 3

Meera 8

11 🔊 Listen to the story.

12 🔊💬 Listen and say the number.

2 My school

1 Listen and point.

chair
book
table
eraser
pencil
pen

2 Listen and repeat.

3 **Say the chant.**

4 **Listen and correct.**

Four purple chairs.

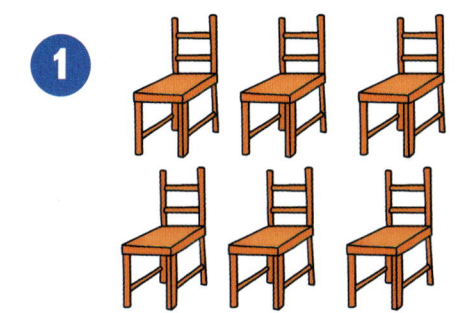

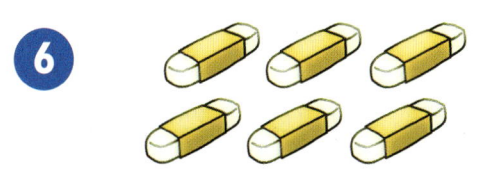

No. Six orange chairs.

Vocabulary

book   chair   eraser   pen   pencil   table

11

5 🎧 Listen and point.

Who's that?

That's Meera. She's eight.

Lenny

Alex

6 🎧 Listen and repeat.

Grammar
Who's that?   He's …   She's …

7 Make the puppets.

8 Sing the song.

Functions

How are you?   I'm fine, thank you.

13

9 Monty's phonics

pink

blue

A **p**ink **p**en and a **b**lue **b**ag.

10 Ask and answer.

Who's that? He's Mr Star.

1 2 3 4
5 6 7 8

11 🔊 Listen to the story.

12 👤💬 Act out the story.

Marie's maths — Adding

1 🔍💬 Look and say the number.

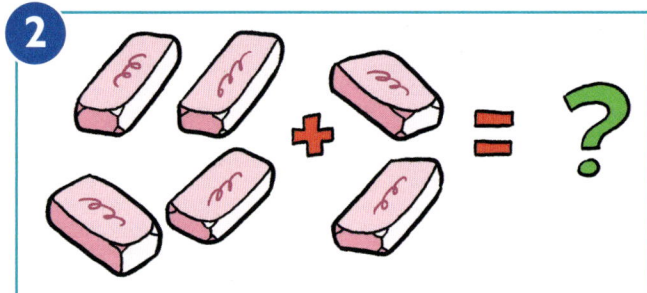

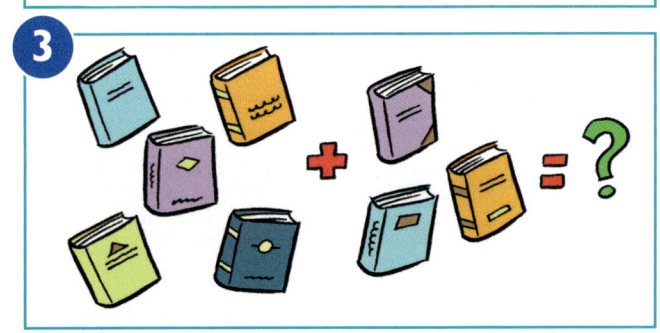

1.
2.
3.
4.

2 🎧 Listen, point and say.

Now you!
Activity Book page 16

Make friends — Trevor's values

3 🔊 Listen to the story.

4 🔊 💬 Listen and say the number. Act it out.

Functions

Great!   Come on! Let's play.   OK.

17

3 Favourite toys

1 🎧 CD1 36 💬 Listen and point.

- doll
- computer
- ball
- car
- train
- bike

2 🎧 CD1 37 💬 Listen and repeat.

3 🔊 💬 Listen and say the number.

1
2
3
4
5
6

4 🔊 💬 Say the chant.

Vocabulary
ball   bike   car   computer   doll   train   black   brown   grey   white

19

5 🎵42 CD1 👤 Listen and do the actions.

Is your ball in your bag?

No, it's next to your chair.

6 🎵43 CD1 💬 Listen and repeat.

Grammar
It's in / next to / on / under …

20

7 🎵 Sing the song.

8 💬 Ask and answer.

Is Monty under the chair?

No, he isn't.

21

9 Monty's phonics

train

doll

Ten dolls on a train.

10 Hide and play.

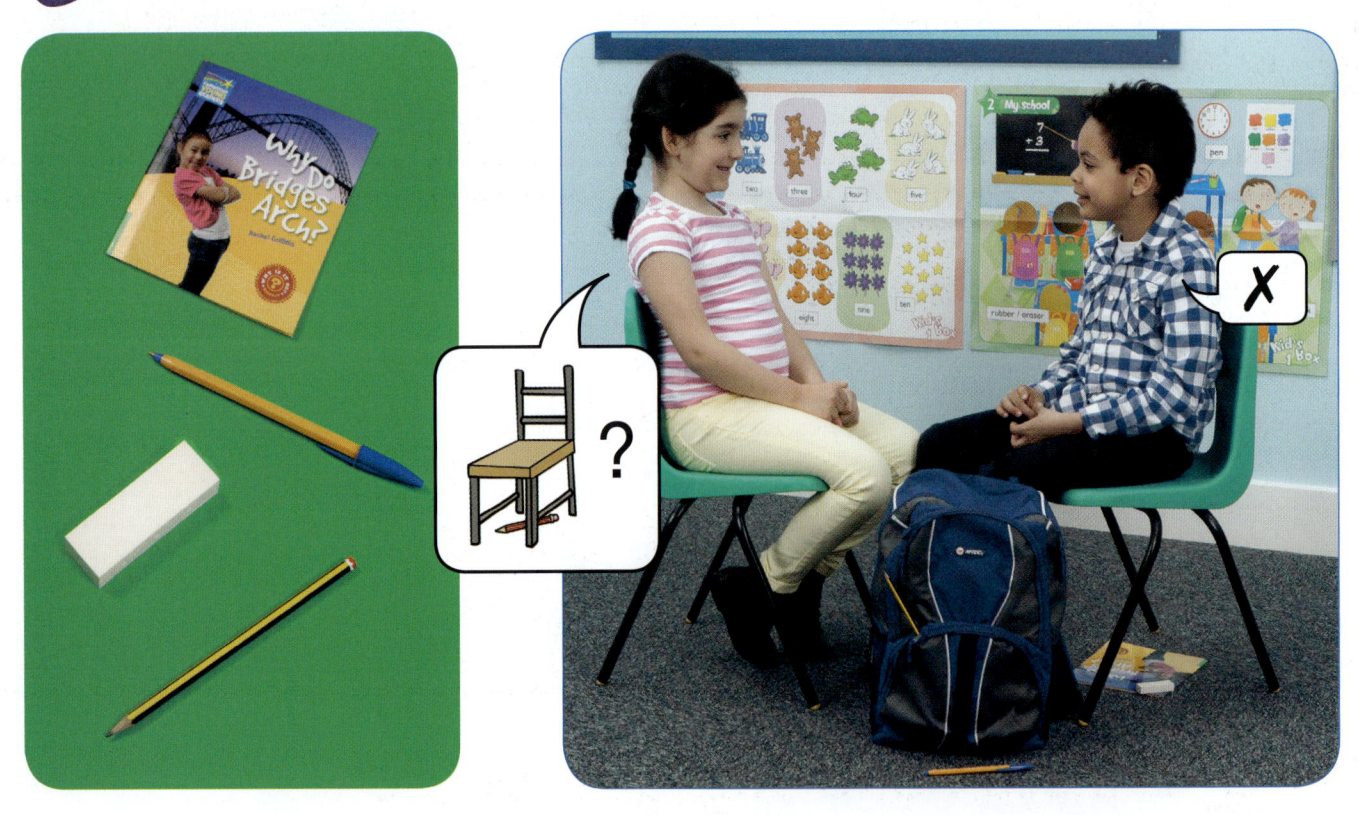

11 🔊 51 CD1 Listen to the story.

12 🔊 52 CD1 💬 Listen and say 'yes' or 'no'.

23

4 My family

1 Listen and point.

- grandfather
- grandmother
- brother
- sister
- father
- mother

2 Listen and repeat.

3 Listen and say the number.

4 Look, listen and say the words.

Vocabulary

brother   sister   father   mother   grandfather   grandmother

25

5 🔊 Listen and point.

- sad
- beautiful
- ugly
- old
- happy
- young

6 🔊 Listen and do the actions.

Grammar
He's / She's beautiful / ugly / happy / sad / old / young.

7 🎵 Sing the song.

8 💬 Listen and chant.

9 Monty's phonics

s**a**d

h**a**ppy

S**a**d c**a**t. H**a**ppy c**a**t!

10 Listen and correct.

Look at my mother. She's ugly.

No, she isn't. She's beautiful.

11 🔊 Listen to the story.

12 🔊 💬 Listen and say the number.

Marie's art — Mixing colours

1 🔊 💬 Listen and say.

2 💬 👥 Look and guess. Do.

What's blue and red?

Purple!

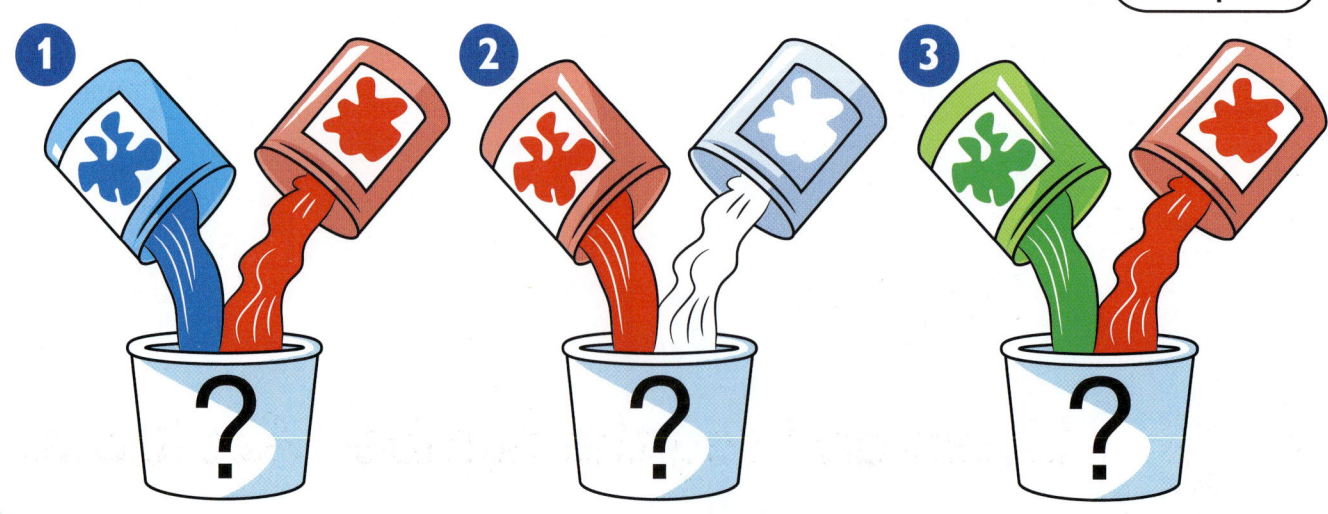

Now you!
Activity Book page 30

Be kind | **Trevor's values**

3 🔊 Listen to the story.

4 🔊 💬 Listen and say the number. Act it out.

Functions

Here you are.   Thanks.   I'm sorry.   That's OK.

31

Review

1 🔊 Listen and say the number.

2 💬 Say and guess.

It's green.
It's on a chair.

Number nine.

3 🎧 CD2 25 👥 Listen and colour. Make a spinner.

4 👥 Play the game.

5 Our pets

1 🎧 26 CD2 👆 Listen and point.

horse

fish

mouse

cat

bird

dog

2 🎧 27 CD2 💬 Listen and repeat.

3 🔊 CD2 29 💬 Say the chant.

4 🔊 CD2 30 💬 Listen and say the number.

Vocabulary
bird   cat   dog   fish   horse   mouse

Grammar
They're …

35

5 🔊 31 CD2 👂 Listen and point.

dirty
long
clean
small
big
short

6 🔊 32 CD2 💬 Listen and repeat.

36 | Grammar
It's / They're big / small / clean / dirty / long / short.

7 🎧 34 CD2 👤 Listen and do the actions.

8 🎧 35 CD2 🎵 Sing the song.

9 Monty's phonics

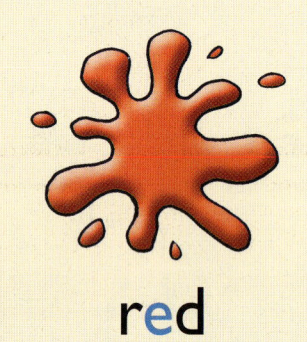

10
ten

red

Ten red pets.

10 Say and guess.

They're long and ugly.

Number six. The fish.

1
2
3
4
5
6
7
8

11 🔊 Listen to the story.

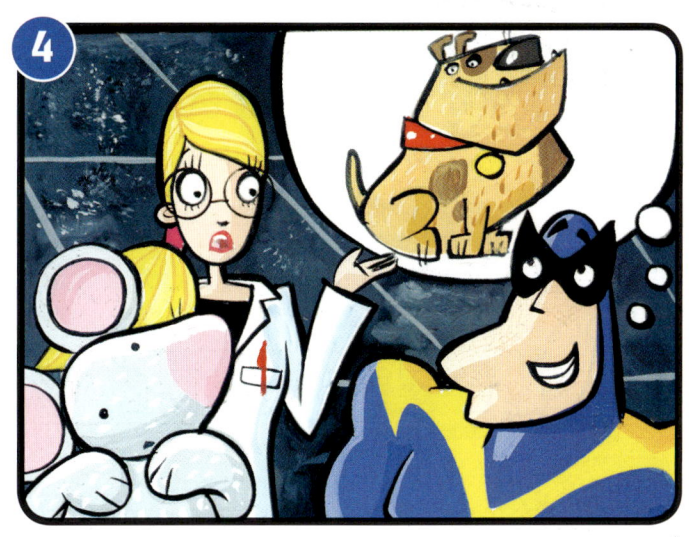

12 👤💬 Act out the story.

6 My face

1 🎧 Listen and point.

- ear
- hair
- eye
- face
- nose
- teeth
- mouth

2 🎧 Listen and repeat.

3 🔊 43 CD2 💬 Say the chant.

4 🔊 44 CD2 💬 Listen and correct.

I'm a boy monster.

No. She's a girl monster.

Vocabulary

ears   eyes   face   hair   mouth   nose   teeth

41

5 🎵 46 CD2 👂 Listen and point.

"I've got a yellow face."

6 🎵 47 CD2 💬 Listen and repeat.

Grammar
I've got …   Have you got … ?   Yes, I have.   No, I haven't.

7 🎵 Sing the song.

8 💬 ✏️ Say and listen. Draw.

I'm a very ugly monster. I've got three eyes.

9 Monty's phonics

green

brown

frog

A **gr**een and **br**own **fr**og.

10 Play the game. Ask and guess.

"Have you got a brown dog?" "Yes, I have."

1.
2.
3.
4.

11 🔊 Listen to the story.

12 🔊💬 Listen and say 'yes' or 'no'.

Marie's science — The senses

1 🎧 Listen and point.

2 👉 Point and say the sense.

Vocabulary: hear   see   smell   taste   touch

Now you!
Activity Book page 46

Look after pets — Trevor's values

3 🎧 💬 Listen and say the number.

1.
2.
3.
4.

4 🧒💬 Do the actions. Guess.

Vocabulary
brush feed walk wash

47

7 Wild animals

1 🎵 CD3 2 💬 **Listen and point.**

- giraffe
- elephant
- snake
- crocodile
- monkey
- hippo
- tiger

2 🎵 CD3 3 💬 **Listen and repeat.**

48

3 🔊 CD3 5 👤 Say the chant. Do the actions.

4 🔊 CD3 6 👂 Listen and point. Answer.

Vocabulary

crocodile   elephant   giraffe   hippo   monkey   snake   tiger

5 🎧 Listen and point.

foot
hand
leg
arm
tail
feet

They've got big ears.

6 🎧 Listen and repeat.

Grammar
They've got / They haven't got arms / feet / hands / legs / tails.

7 🔟 🎵 Sing the song.

8 🧑 💬 Act it out and say.

What am I? You're an elephant.

9 Monty's phonics

fish

big

Six big fish.

10 Play the game. Ask and answer.

Have they got small ears?

No, they haven't.

big / small	heads, ears, feet, mouths
short / long	tails, noses, legs, arms

11 🎧 Listen to the story.

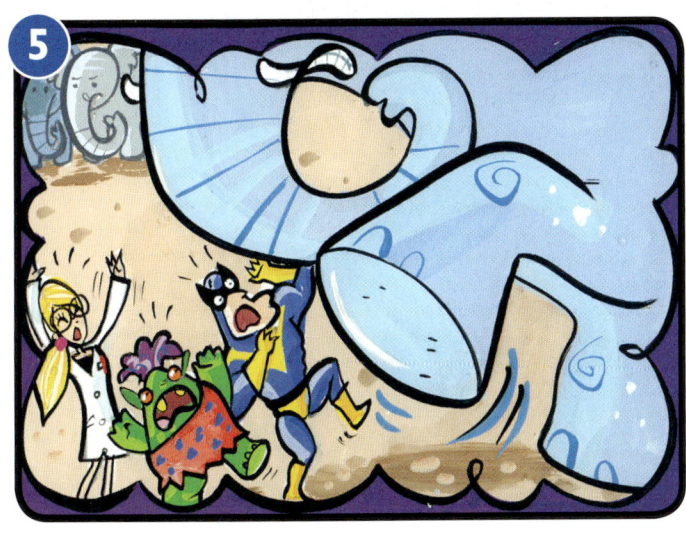

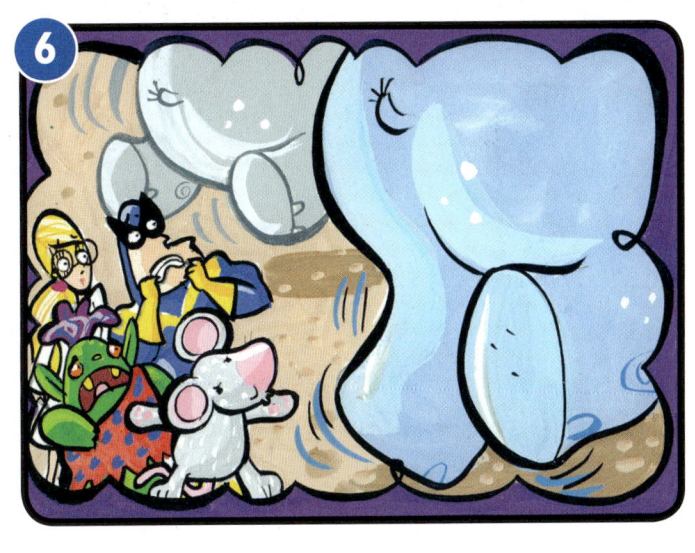

12 🧍💬 Act out the story.

8 My clothes

1 🎧 15 CD3 👂 **Listen and point.**

- T-shirt
- skirt
- socks
- jacket
- shoes
- trousers

2 🎧 16 CD3 💬 **Listen and repeat.**

3 🔊 18 CD3 💬 Say the chant.

4 🔊 19 CD3 💬 Listen and say the number.

1 2 3 4

Vocabulary

jacket   shoes   skirt   socks   trousers   T-shirt

55

5 🎧 Listen and point.

"Has Simon got my red trousers?"

6 🎧 Listen and repeat.

Grammar
He's / She's got …   He / She hasn't got …

7 🔊 💬 Listen and correct.

8 🔊 🎵 Sing the song.

9 **Monty's phonics**

orange

socks   dog

A long dog in orange socks.

10 Ask and answer.

She's got a yellow jacket.

Meera!

11 🔊 Listen to the story.

12 🔊💬 Listen and say the number.

Marie's geography — Habitats

1 🎧 Listen and point.

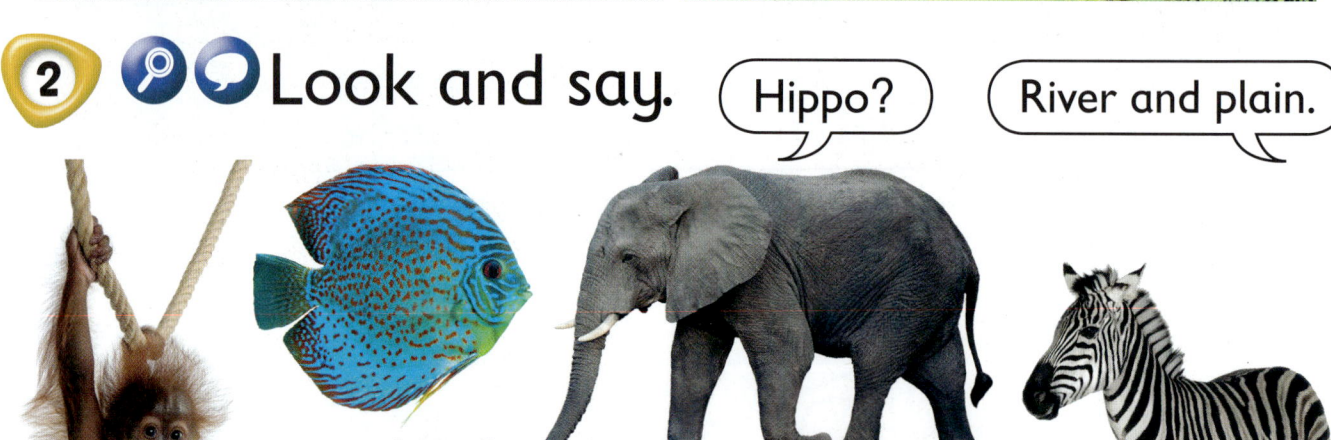

1. plain / river
2. forest

2 🔍💬 Look and say.

— Hippo?
— River and plain.

Vocabulary: forest plain river

Now you!
Activity Book page 60

Love nature — Trevor's values

3 🔊 Listen to the story.

1
2
3
4

4 🔊 💬 Listen. Say 'happy' or 'sad'.

Review

1 🎧 💬 Listen and say the number.

2 🔍 💬 Look, read and match.

It's a hippo.

zebra   hippo   elephant   crocodile

3 👥💬 Play the game. Say the words.

9 Fun time!

1 🎧 CD3 38 👆 Listen and point.

- play the piano
- play basketball
- play the guitar
- play tennis
- swim
- play football
- ride a bike

2 🎧 CD3 39 💬 Listen and repeat.

3 🎧 41 CD3 💬 Listen and answer.

4 🎧 42 CD3 🎵 Sing the song.

Vocabulary
play basketball / football / tennis   play the guitar / piano   swim   ride a bike

65

5 🎧 44 CD3 👂 Listen and point.

I can't sing.

I can ride a bike.

She can ride a horse.

6 🎧 45 CD3 💬 Listen and repeat.

Grammar
I / You / He / She can ...   I / You / He / She can't ...

7 Say the chant.

8 Listen and answer.

Who can draw? Grandma.

9 Monty's phonics

Lily

blue

Lily's got a blue and yellow tail.

10 Ask and answer.

Can you sing?
Yes, I can.
Can you swim?
No, I can't.

11 🎧 Listen to the story.

12 👥💬 Act out the story.

10 At the funfair

1 🎧 Listen and point.

lorry
motorbike
plane
boat
bus
helicopter

2 🎧 💬 Listen and repeat.

3 Say the chant. Do the actions.

4 Listen and answer.

Is the red car in the shoe?

Yes, it is.

Vocabulary

boat   bus   helicopter   lorry   motorbike   plane   ship

5 🎵 CD4 👂 Listen and point.

"What are you doing, Maskman?"

"I'm flying my plane."

6 🎵 CD4 💬 Listen and repeat.

Grammar
What are you doing?   I'm driving / flying / riding / walking.

7 🎵 Sing the song.

8 Do the actions. Play the game.

What am I doing?   You're driving a lorry.

9 Monty's phonics

d**u**ck

under

b**u**s

The d**u**cks are **u**nder the b**u**s.

10 Listen and correct.

I'm driving my car.

No, you're walking.

1
2
3
4
5
6

11 🔊 Listen to the story.

12 🔊💬 Listen and say the number.

Marie's sports — Things for sports

1 🔊 💬 **Listen and say.**

> They're sailing.

playing basketball   playing table-tennis
riding bikes   riding horses   sailing

1.
2.
3.
4.
5.

2 💬 **Say and answer.**

> They've got a big orange ball.

> They're playing basketball.

Vocabulary
play table-tennis   sail

Now you!
Activity Book page 76

Work in teams — Trevor's values

3 🔊 Listen to the story.

4 💬 Listen and say the number. Act it out.

Functions
I can help you. Work in teams.

77

11 Our house

1 🔊 Listen and point.

bedroom

bathroom

living room

dining room

kitchen

hall

2 🔊 Listen and repeat.

3 🎧 CD4 24 💬 **Listen and correct.**

"Monty's in the bathroom."

"No, he isn't. He's in the bedroom."

4 🎧 CD4 25 💬 **Listen and answer.**

"Where's the computer?"

"It's in the kitchen."

Vocabulary

bathroom   bedroom   dining room   hall   kitchen   living room

79

5 🎧 CD4 26 👂 Listen and point.

What's Simon doing?

He's drawing a picture.

6 🎧 CD4 27 💬 Listen and repeat.

Grammar
What's he / she doing?   He's / She's ...ing

7 🎵 Sing the song.

8 💬 Ask and answer.

What's Stella doing?

She's reading a book.

Where is she?

She's in the bedroom.

9 Monty's phonics

horse

hippo

A **h**orse and a **h**ippo in a **h**elicopter.

10 Say and guess.

playing   driving   flying   eating
reading   playing   swimming   watching

They're eating fish.

Number four.

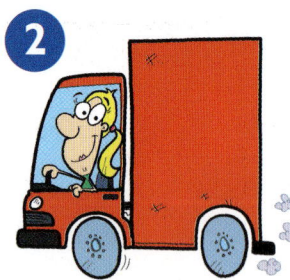

1
2
3
4
5
6
7
8

11 🎧 **Listen to the story.**

12 🎧 💬 **Listen and say 'yes' or 'no'.**

12 Party time!

1 🎧 35 CD4 👁 Listen and point.

- ice cream
- apple
- banana
- cake
- chocolate
- burger

2 🎧 36 CD4 💬 Listen and repeat.

3 🎧38 💬 Say the chant.

4 🎧39 💬 Listen and say 'yes' or 'no'.

Vocabulary

apple   banana   burger   cake   chocolate   ice cream   kiwi   orange

5 🔊 Listen and point.

"I like chocolate cake."

"I don't like chocolate."

"Do you like Maskman cake?"

6 🔊 Listen and repeat.

Grammar
I like ...   I don't like ...   Do you like ... ?

7 🎵 Sing the song.

8 💬 Ask and answer.

- Do you like apples?
- Yes, I do.
- Do you like ice cream?
- No, I don't.

Monty's phonics

pie

like

white

bike

I like my white bike!

10 Read. Listen and say the name.

Sam: I like  🏀 and ⚽, but I don't like 🏊 or 🎾.

Sue: I don't like  🐕 or 🐎, but I like 🐈 and 🐦.

May: I like  👗 and 🧥, but I don't like 👖 or 👕.

Ben: I don't like 🥧 or 🍫, but I like 🍦 and 🥪.

11 🔊 Listen to the story.

12 🧍💬 Act out the story.

Marie's art — Fruit in paintings

1 👂💬 Point and say the food.

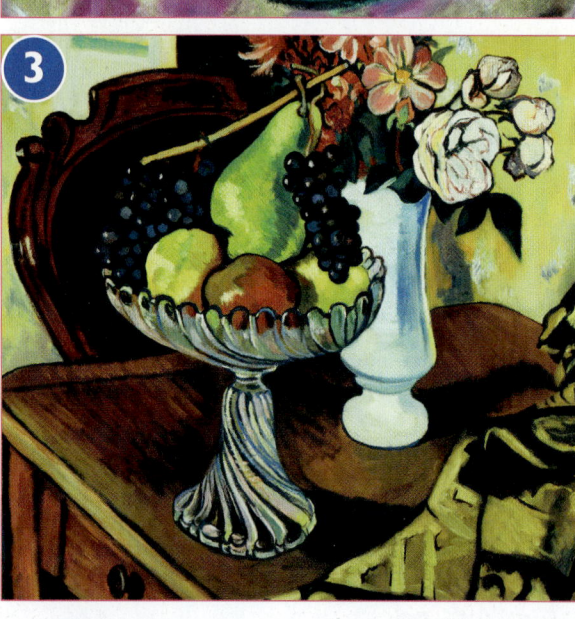

1

2

3

4

2 🔊 CD4 50 💬 Listen and say the number.

90

Vocabulary

painting   grapes   lemon   pear   watermelon

Now you!
Activity Book page 90

Keep clean — Trevor's values

3 🎧 51 CD4 — Listen and point.

4 🎧 52 CD4 💬 Say the chant. Do the actions.

Vocabulary
clean your teeth   wash apples   wash your hands

Review

9 10 11 12

1 🎧 💬 Listen and answer.

2 🔍 Read.

I'm Ben. I'm **7**. I like ⚽ and 🏐, but I don't like 🎾. I can 🏊 and ride a 🚲, but I can't play the 🎸. I like 🍰 and 🍔, but I don't like 🍫 or 🍦. I like 🍏 and 🥝. I'm eating a 🍌 now.

92

3 👥💬 Play the game. Say.

> The elephant's drinking water.

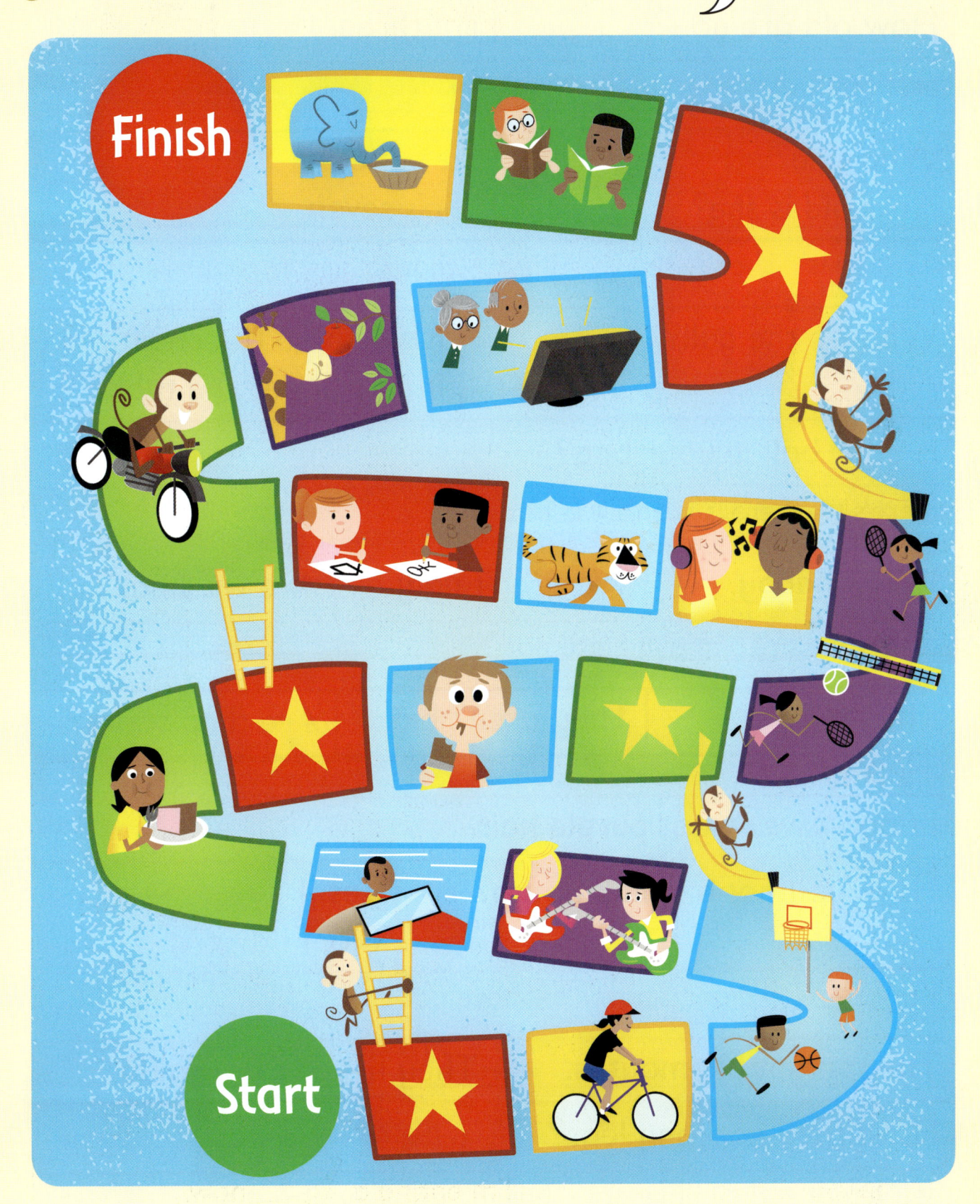

Grammar reference

1
| What's your name? | I'm Suzy. |
| How old are you? | I'm three. |

I'm = I am

2
| Who's he? | He's Alex. |
| How old is she? | She's seven. |

he's = he is   she's = she is   that's = that is

3
Where's the ball?	It's next to the chair.
	It isn't under the table.
Is your ball in your bag?	

where's = where is   isn't = is not

4
| We're happy. | We aren't ugly. | Are we small? |

we're = we are   aren't = are not

5
| They're long. | They aren't big. | Are they short? |

6
I / you / we've got purple hair.	
Have you got a small mouth?	Yes, I have.
	No, I haven't.

I've got = I have got   haven't = have not

7
| They've got big mouths. | They haven't got tails. |
| Have they got long legs? | |

they've got = they have got   haven't got = have not got

94

8

She's got your red trousers.	He hasn't got a white ball.
Has he/she got a train?	Yes, he/she has. No, he/she hasn't.

he's got = he has got   she's got = she has got
hasn't got = has not got

9

I ...	can can't	sing. play the guitar.
Can you ride a bike?		

can't = cannot

10

What are you doing?	I'm flying.
Are you flying your helicopter?	

11

What's he/she doing? What are they doing?	He's/She's listening to music. They're sitting on the sofa.
Is he/she listening to music?	Yes, he/she is. No, he/she isn't.

what's = what is

12

I like cake.	I don't like chocolate.
Do you like snakes?	Yes, I do. No, I don't.

don't = do not

Thanks and Acknowledgements

Authors' thanks

Many thanks to everyone at Cambridge University Press and in particular to:

Rosemary Bradley for supervising the whole project and for her keen editorial eye;
Emily Hird for her energy, enthusiasm and enormous organisational capacity;
Colin Sage for his hard work, good ideas and helpful suggestions;
Claire Appleyard for her editorial contribution.

Many thanks to Karen Elliott for her expertise and enthusiasm in the writing of the Phonics sections.

We would also like to thank all our pupils and colleagues at Star English, El Palmar, Murcia and especially Jim Kelly and Julie Woodman for their help and suggestions at various stages of the project.

Dedications

I would like to dedicate this book to the women who have been my pillars of strength: Milagros Marín, Sara de Alba, Elia Navarro and Maricarmen Balsalobre - CN

To Paloma, for her love, encouragement and unwavering support. Thanks. - MT

The Authors and Publishers would like to thank the following teachers for their help in reviewing the material and for the invaluable feedback they provided:

Luciana Pittondo, Soledad Gimenez, Argentina; Gan Ping, Zou Yang, China; Keily Duran, Colombia; Elvia Gutierrez Reyes, Yadira Hernandez, Mexico; Rachel Lunan, Russia; Lorraine Mealing, Sharon Hopkins, Spain; Inci Kartal, Turkey.

The authors and publishers would like to thank the following consultants for their invaluable input:

Coralyn Bradshaw, Helen Chilton, Marla Del Signore, Pippa Mayfield, Hilary Ratcliff, Lynne Rushton, Melanie Williams.

We would also like to thank all the teachers who allowed us to observe their classes, and who gave up their invaluable time for interviews and focus groups.

The authors and publishers acknowledge the following sources of copyright material and are grateful for the permissions granted. While every effort has been made, it has not always been possible to identify the sources of all the material used, or to trace all copyright holders. If any omissions are brought to our notice, we will be happy to include the appropriate acknowledgements on reprinting.

t = top, c = centre, b = below, l = left, r = right

p. 17 (t): Thinkstock; p. 31 (t): Thinkstock; p. 47 (t): Thinkstock; p. 60 (tl): Shutterstock.com/Gualtiero Boffi; p. 60 (tr, bc): Shutterstock/Eric Isselee; p. 60 (bl): Getty Images/iStock/GlobalP; p. 60 (br): Shutterstock/Ekaterina V. Borisova; p. 60 (tc): Shutterstock/defpicture; p. 61 (t): Thinkstock; p. 62 (l): Shutterstock/MIMOHE; p. 62 (r): Shutterstock/Jiri Foltyn; p. 62 (cl): Shutterstock/Jassam; p. 62 (cr): Getty Images/The Image Bank/James Warwick; p. 76 (tl): Getty Images/AFP/TORU YAMANAKA; p. 76 (cl): Alamy/©Kuttig – People; p. 76 (br): Getty Images/Getty Images Sport/Tim Nwachukwu; p. 76 (bl): Getty Images/Onne van der Wal/The Image Bank; p 76 (tr): Superstock/Juniors; p. 77 (t): Thinkstock; p. 90 (tr, bl): SuperStock/Christie's Images Ltd; p. 90 (tl): Superstock/Leslie Hinrichs; p. 90 (br): Superstock/Peter Willi; p. 91 (t): Thinkstock.

Commissioned photography on pages 13, 21, 22, 32, 33, 43, 52, 68, 81 by Trevor Clifford Photography.

The authors and publishers are grateful to the following illustrators:

Beatrice Costamagna, c/o Pickled ink; Chris Garbutt, c/o Arena; Lucía Serrano Guerroro; Andrew Hennessey; Kelly Kennedy, c/o Syvlie Poggio; Rob McKlurkan, c/o The Bright Agency; Melanie Sharp, c/o Syvlie Poggio; Marie Simpson, c/o Pickled ink; Emily Skinner, c/o Graham-Cameron Illustration; Lisa Smith; Gary Swift; Lisa Williams, c/o Syvlie Poggio;

The publishers are grateful to the following contributors:

Louise Edgeworth: art direction
Hilary Fletcher: picture research
Wild Apple Design Ltd: page design
Blooberry: additional design
Lon Chan: cover design
Melanie Sharp: cover illustration
John Green and Tim Woolf, TEFL Audio: audio recordings
Robert Lee: song writing
hyphen S.A.: editorial management